Bodies of Water

Oceans

A 4D BOOK

by Erika L. Shores

PEBBLE
a capstone imprint

Download the Capstone 4D app!

- Ask an adult to download the Capstone 4D app.
- Scan the cover and stars inside the book for additional content.

When you scan a spread, you'll find fun extra stuff to go with this book! You can also find these things on the web at www.capstone4D.com using the password: oceans.14650

Little Pebble is published by Pebble
1710 Roe Crest Drive, North Mankato,
Minnesota 56003
www.mycapstone.com

Library of Congress Cataloging-in-Publication Data
Library of Congress Cataloging-in-Publication Data is available on the Library of Congress website.
ISBN: 978-1-5435-1465-0 (library binding)
— 978-1-5435-1469-8 (paperback) —
978-1-5435-1473-5 (ebook PDF)

Editorial Credits
Bobbie Nuytten, designer; Morgan Walters, media researcher; Tori Abraham, production specialist

Photo Credits
Newscom: QAI Publishing Universal Images Group, 11; Shutterstock: Baoyan zeng, Cover, 1, Dmitry Pichugin, 5, GaudiLab, 9, Maen Zayyad, 21, Marina Ivanova, 7, Proskurina Yuliya, (wave) design element, Rich Carey, 17, Sergey Uryadnikov, 15, Sukhum Klatalumbon, 13, worldswildlifewonders, 19

Printed and bound in China.
000309

Table of Contents

What Is an Ocean?

An ocean is a body of water.

The water is salty.

There are five oceans.

The Pacific Ocean

is the biggest.

Ocean water meets land.

This is called the coast.

Parts of oceans are
very deep.
The ocean floor
is dark and cold.

ocean
floor

What Is in an Ocean?

Splash!

Dolphins leap.

Chomp!

Sharks bite.

They eat other fish.

Seaweed grows

in sunny water.

Kelp grows tall and thick.

Look!

Sea otters lay in it.

kelp

People and Oceans

People live by oceans.

They swim and play.

Glossary

coast—land next to an ocean

dolphin—a water mammal with a long snout

kelp—a large, brown seaweed

sea otter—a furry mammal that lives along the coasts of the Pacific Ocean; sea otters rest in kelp so that they don't float away.

seaweed—a plant that grows underwater

Read More

Holland, Simon. *Oceans: Can You Tell the Facts from the Fibs?* North Mankato, Minn.: Capstone Press, 2016.

Sullivan, Laura L. *24 Hours in the Ocean.* A Day in an Ecosystem. New York: Cavendish Square Publishing, 2018.

Wilsdon, Christina. *Ultimate Oceanpedia: The Most Complete Ocean Reference Ever.* Washington, D.C.: National Geographic Children's Books, 2016.

Internet Sites

Use FactHound to find Internet sites related to this book.

Visit www.facthound.com

Just type in 9781543514650 and go.

Super-cool stuff!

Check out projects, games and lots more at
www.capstonekids.com

Critical Thinking Questions

1. What is the land that meets the ocean called?

2. Why are oceans important to animals?

3. Which ocean is the world's biggest?

Index

Bodies of Water

Oceans hold salt water.
Read about these huge
bodies of water.

Titles in this set:
Lakes
Oceans
Ponds
Rivers

A **4D** BOOK

Check out Capstone 4D
for a cool video and more!

F&P Text Level Gradient™
Officially Leveled by **Fountas & Pinnell**

ATOS: 1.0

RL: K-1 IL: PreK-2
ISBN 978-1-5435-1469-8

9 781543 514698

90000

capstone
www.mycapstone.com

O8-AAP-574

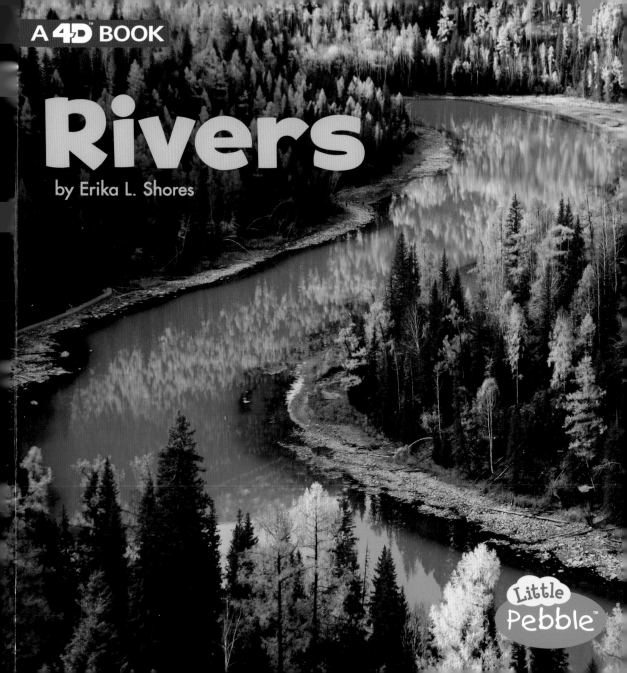

A **4D** BOOK

Rivers
by Erika L. Shores

Little Pebble